GLORY DAYS

BET Group

BEST ▶▶▶ GIFTS ▶▶▶ FASTER save GREEN SHIELD

93 KIDLINGTON ST'N

331

331 RJO

Ian Allan PUBLISHING

Gavin Booth

Front cover:
Typical of many single-deck buses supplied to BET Group companies in the late 1950s/early 1960s —South Wales No 825 (XWN 802), a 1961 AEC Reliance 2MU3RV with 45-seat Park Royal body, photographed in Llanelli in July 1963. *P. R. Wallis*

Back cover:
Southdown was always one of the most charismatic BET companies, and its immaculate green/cream buses suited its operating area in Sussex. No 782 (RUF 182) is a 1956 Leyland Titan PD2/12 with stylish Beadle 59-seat body, seen at Brighton's Pool Valley bus station. *Roy Marshall/ Photobus*

Title page:
Unusual purchases for City of Oxford were short-length (27ft 6in) AEC Renown 3B3RAs with Park Royal 65-seat forward-entrance bodies. No 331 (331 RJO), new in 1963, is seen in 1964; alongside is a Willowbrook-bodied AEC Reliance. *R. G. Funnell*

Contents

First published 1998

ISBN 0 7110 2609 2

Published by Ian Allan Publishing

an imprint of Ian Allan Publishing Ltd, Terminal House, Station Approach, Shepperton, Surrey TW17 8AS.
Printed by Ian Allan Printing Ltd, Riverdene Business Park, Molesey Road, Hersham, Surrey KT12 4RG.

Code: 9810/B2

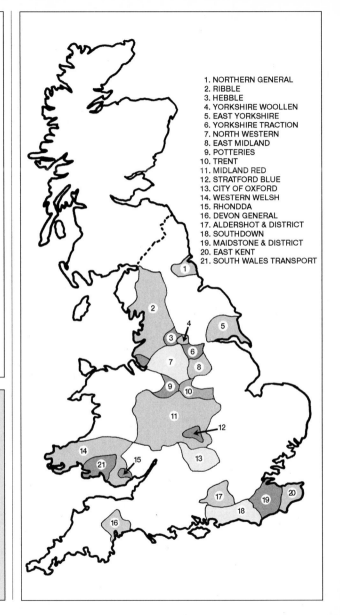

1. NORTHERN GENERAL
2. RIBBLE
3. HEBBLE
4. YORKSHIRE WOOLLEN
5. EAST YORKSHIRE
6. YORKSHIRE TRACTION
7. NORTH WESTERN
8. EAST MIDLAND
9. POTTERIES
10. TRENT
11. MIDLAND RED
12. STRATFORD BLUE
13. CITY OF OXFORD
14. WESTERN WELSH
15. RHONDDA
16. DEVON GENERAL
17. ALDERSHOT & DISTRICT
18. SOUTHDOWN
19. MAIDSTONE & DISTRICT
20. EAST KENT
21. SOUTH WALES TRANSPORT

Introduction

Throughout the 26-year period from 1942 to 1968, when the British bus industry reached its peak, there were four main groups of operators dominating the scene. There were the corporation fleets, which had usually started with tramcars, before moving on to motorbuses, and sometimes trolleybuses; there were the nationalised groupings, from 1948-9 — the Tilling Group, the SMT/Scottish Group and London Transport; there were the privately-owned independents, ranging in size from just one bus to over 450; and there was the BET Group, with a significant proportion of its shares held by the state, but with a fiercely independent, profit-centred attitude to ownership. While the corporation and nationalised fleets were strong on the concept of public service, even at the expense of profits, BET believed in public service *and* profitability. In 1990s terms, the BET Group could be compared with the Stagecoach empire.

BET stood for British Electric Traction, and this provides a major clue to the group's roots. While the Tilling and Scottish groups were largely based on pioneering bus operations, BET, like the corporations, was firmly based on the electric tramcar, though as we shall discover the far-sighted businessmen who guided BET were not so blinkered that they ignored the new-fangled motorbus. What at one time appeared to be a threat to the tramway systems, was quickly seen to be a means to provide links that would be expensive by tram, and, gradually, as the motorbus became more sophisticated and economical, it was recognised that this was where the future lay.

Where the Tilling Group companies were perceived as solid and dependable, with a high degree of centralised control and standardisation, the BET Group companies were often more charismatic, with, perhaps, more concern for the bottom line, where managers were allowed to follow individual paths as long as the companies achieved the desired levels of profitability. You only have to look at companies like Midland Red, Ribble and Southdown to recognise the individuality, or at adjacent companies like South Wales and Western Welsh to realise that belonging to a group did not mean that everything had to be the same.

This book concentrates on the period from 1942 — the birth of the BET Group that most readers will remember — through to the sell-off to the state in 1968, which allowed the

Government to lay the foundations of what became the National Bus Company, before a further change of political direction led to privatisation in the 1980s, and the dismantling of groupings that had been slowly forming since the early years of the 20th century.

Readers interested in other BET Group companies may wish to buy the companion title *Glory Days: Midland Red* which deals at greater length with the Midland Red company, and the history of the Tilling group is covered in another title in the series, *Glory Days: Tilling Group*.

Gavin Booth
Edinburgh

One of BET's first ventures into motorbus operation was in Birmingham, and although this was initially unsuccessful, the Birmingham & Midland Motor Omnibus Co Ltd grew to become the largest company bus fleet in England and Wales. The company, usually known as Midland Red, was remarkable in that it designed and built its own buses, mainly for its own use, but at one stage for fellow BET companies. This BMMO-built D7 type double-decker, 4382 (VHA 382) was new in 1955 with Metro-Cammell 63-seat body. It is seen in Shrewsbury in 1969. *Arnold Richardson/Photobus*

South Wales Transport was a
BET company, even in the
days of T&BAT. It was
famous for its large fleet of
AECs, like No 1197
(MCY 418), a 1955 Regent V
with lowbridge 56-seat Metro-
Cammell bodywork, seen in
Ammanford in 1962.
Roy Marshall/Photobus

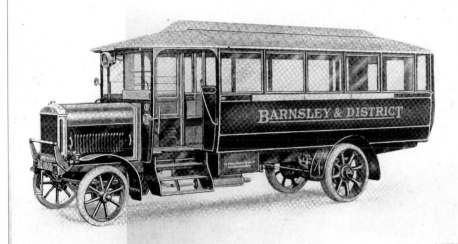

An early normal-control Leyland N type with Strachan & Brown body (HE 1808) for the Barnsley & District company, predecessor of Yorkshire Traction. *Ian Allan Library*

1. From Tramcars to Motorbuses

In the closing years of the 19th century the electric tramcar was seen as the most efficient form of urban transportation. It would be some years before the internal combustion engine would start to make any real impact on the world of private transport, and though motorbuses were not far behind, they were crude and basic compared with the smooth and quiet electric tramcar which was to hold sway in Britain's towns and cities well into the 20th century.

The man who formed the British Electric Traction Co Ltd (BET) in 1895, Emile Garcke, could not know what was coming. His expertise was in electrical engineering and he recognised the potential that existed for taking over existing tramways to electrify them, setting up new tramway systems, and creating electricity-generating concerns that could supply power for the trams and for general customers. BET found itself involved in bus operation at an early stage and while initially it saw the bus as a feeder to its tramway systems, it was not blind to its potential. As buses became more refined, and offered a realistic and economic alternative to the tramcar, BET became more heavily involved in the bus business.

From the start, BET was a vocal opponent of the Tramways Act of 1870 which meant that local authorities could own, but not operate, tramways, and had the right of compulsory purchase after 21 years. For a commercially driven company like BET this had no great attraction, and the Light Railways Act of 1896, which offered greater security of tenure, was the signal for BET and other groups to proceed with electrification more confidently.

BET dabbled in motorbuses with varying degrees of success, in the Potteries, in Birmingham and, more notably, in Kent. Emile Garcke's son, Sidney, set up Deal & District Motor Services in 1908, using buses that had formerly run in Birmingham.

In London BET had two tramway companies: Metropolitan Electric Tramways (MET) and the South Metropolitan company. These were essentially suburban tramways, but when the buses of the powerful London General Omnibus Company (LGOC) started to operate beyond the previous 15-mile radius from central London, BET recognised the threat to its trams. It countered by forming the Tramways (MET) Omnibus Company and placing a substantial order for 100 Daimler buses. LGOC countered with an order for 250 Daimlers, which was topped by a BET order for 350. But before a bus war broke out, LGOC and BET reached an agreement which limited LGOC's operating area and restricted the number of BET buses in London. Something similar had already happened with Thomas Tilling and over a number of years these agreements led to the situation where LGOC and its successors had a virtual monopoly in London, and BET and Tilling dominated the provision of bus services throughout much of England and Wales. In Scotland, in a parallel development, the Scottish Motor Traction company (SMT) emerged as the basis of an important group, covering much of the country.

An early indication of BET's interest in motorbuses had been the creation of the British Automobile Development company in 1905 — from 1912 the British Automobile Traction company (BAT) — which was destined to become a major player in the British bus industry.

BAT and Tilling, unable to expand in London, both looked to Kent in the years around World War 1. There was Sidney Garcke's Deal & District company, and other local firms acquired by BAT, and there was Tilling's Folkestone District company. In 1916 these companies were merged to form the East Kent Road Car company, with BAT and Tilling each holding an interest — the start of a pattern that would allow the industry to develop at a greater pace.

Along the south coast in Sussex, Tilling and BAT found themselves competing for business in the Brighton area, through tramway and motorbus companies they had acquired, but further acquisitions led to the formation of Southdown Motor Services, which ultimately would be one of the best-loved BET companies, and the Tilling operation was eventually branded Brighton, Hove & District.

Tilling and BET/BAT were fast emerging as the main territorial operators in England and Wales outside London, and in 1928 Tilling & British Automobile Traction Ltd (T&BAT) was formed to formalise existing relationships between the groups. Tilling had a substantial holding in BAT and the two groups saw the value of working together to present a powerful front that must have deterred other competitors. Not all BET bus companies passed into T&BAT control, and BET held on to direct ownership of some companies, just as Tilling held on to its London and Brighton operations.

As BET developed its bus interests it started to look beyond southeast England. The companies that many readers will remember in the 1950s and 1960s as BET companies came from very different backgrounds. Some had very clear roots in BET's many tramway schemes, and although the generating and use of

Potteries was one of the 'pure' BET fleets, with its BET origins in the Potteries Electric Traction Co in the last years of the 19th century. Intense competition from motorbuses led to the withdrawal of the trams by 1928. This 1960 Leyland Tiger Cub PSUC1/1 with 45-seat Park Royal bus body represents typical BET Group single-deck fare in the late 1950s/early 1960s before 36ft-long buses were sanctioned. It was new to Stratford Blue, passing to Potteries as No 407 (3946 UE) when the Stratford Blue company passed totally into the Midland Red fold. It was photographed, newly repainted, at Stafford in 1971. *Policy Transport Photographs*

Ribble fell into the T&BAT camp until 1942. With its proximity to the Leyland works, it was inevitable that Leyland products should be favoured. No 233 (CRN 983) is a 1949 Leyland Tiger PS2/5 with 35-seat Burlingham bus body. *Tom A. Godfrey*

East Kent, and its neighbours Maidstone & District and Southdown, were T&BAT companies. CFN 123, a Dennis Lancet with rebuilt Park Royal bodywork is seen in July 1968 in Dover, working at the docks, in the shadow of the white cliffs.
R. L. Wilson

electricity was one of BET's primary aims, the company was not slow to convert to motorbuses if this would produce cost savings. Other bus companies were set up by BAT, often to bring together the operations of acquired companies.

The motorbus developed so dramatically in the 1920s that there was pressure to introduce greater controls on this maturing industry. The creation of T&BAT was one recognition of the potential of the bus. The 1930 Road Traffic Act tried to bring order out of confusion, where vehicle, route and crew licensing was haphazard throughout Britain, and there was seen to be a need to regulate the industry before it got out of control. Then there were the four main-line railways, who saw the motorbus as an increasingly serious competitor, and who sought and obtained legislation to allow them to operate bus services. In most cases this was achieved through a shareholding in existing bus companies that was equal to that of the bus company or its holding group. T&BAT was heavily involved in negotiations with the railway companies, and the railway shareholdings allowed them some control over the development of the bus companies, while providing the bus companies with much-needed capital that would see massive investment in new buses, and the consolidation of area companies by a rash of takeovers in the 1930s.

Although the T&BAT companies became involved with the appropriate main-line railway company or companies, there were still the bus companies that remained under BET control — typically those that had begun as tramway companies, and some of these never had any railway involvement.

The T&BAT companies included Aldershot & District, East Kent, East Midland, East Yorkshire, Maidstone & District, North Western, Ribble, Southdown, Trent and Yorkshire Traction. BET retained its direct interests in Midland Red, Northern General, Potteries, South Wales and Yorkshire Woollen.

Other companies joined the fold during the 1930s. BET took over the National Electric Construction company (NEC), another holding and development company, and this brought the City of Oxford, Devon General, Mexborough & Swinton, Rhondda and Western Welsh companies under BET control. The Halifax-based Hebble company had been bought by the London Midland & Scottish railway company (LMS) in 1929, and BET acquired a 50% shareholding in 1932.

In 1942 T&BAT was broken up, and Tilling and BET went their own ways. The trade press at the time explained that the

T&BAT directors 'have now decided that under present conditions a simplification of the present arrangements is desirable; it is considered that greater administrative efficiency will be secured by splitting the company's interests into two parts, with each of the parent companies controlling one part instead of both jointly controlling the whole'. The real reason, it has been suggested, is that the Tilling and BET camps were so different that their senior managers could not continue to work together. Surely a more cordial split would not have taken place at the height of a world war.

Two new companies were set up to run the newly-split companies: Tilling Motor Services and BET Omnibus Services. In most cases the 'obvious' companies went to Tilling and BET, but there were a couple of surprises.

BET took Aldershot & District, East Kent, East Midland, East Yorkshire, Maidstone & District, North Western, Ribble, Southdown, Trent and Yorkshire Traction, which gave it much remunerative territory in southeast England, the East Midlands, Yorkshire and northwest England. East Midland and North Western were surprise additions to the BET camp as these had originally been Tilling companies.

◄◄ Along the coast at Southdown's Portslade works in 1937, with mechanical and body repair work being undertaken on 1930 all-Leyland Titan TD1s. By this time the Southdown fleet had grown to nearly 700 buses and coaches.
Ian Allan Library

▲ The Western Welsh company, passed into BET control in 1931 with the National Electric Construction Group. This 1931 view shows UH 8621, a new AEC Regal with 30-seat rear-entrance Park Royal body, leaving Cardiff for Ammanford.
Ian Allan Library

Maidstone & District favoured Bristol chassis until these were no longer available to non-state-owned fleets. No DH155 (HKE 863) is a 1945 Bristol K6A with a later Weymann 56-seat bodywork, seen in Maidstone in June 1964. *A. J. Douglas/ Photobus*

East Midland was one of the companies that changed allegiance in the 1942 split-up, passing to BET rather than Tilling. No D123 (WAL 123) is a 1957 Leyland Titan PD3/4 with lowbridge Weymann 67-seat bodywork, seen in Doncaster bus station in 1971. *Roy Marshall/ Photobus*

Posed in 1932 near the Loughborough coachworks of Brush, a BET associate company, is Western Welsh No 175 (KG 972), an AEC Regent. *Ian Allan Library*

Tilling took Caledonian, Crosville, Cumberland, Eastern Counties, Hants & Dorset, Lincolnshire, Southern Vectis, Thames Valley, United Auto, West Yorkshire and Wilts & Dorset, which gave it a high proportion of rural and inter-urban work, a situation that was not balanced by the loss of East Midland and North Western and the gaining of the Crosville, Cumberland and Lincolnshire companies from BET.

The BET Group's bus interests were of course much more extensive than the former T&BAT companies, and there were also the directly controlled groupings.

This table (*opposite*) shows the state of the BET Group after the 1942 reorganisation. The railway interests were held by the Great Western Railway (GWR), London & North Eastern Railway (LNER), London, Midland & Scottish Railway (LMS) and Southern Railway (SR).

The BET Group in 1942

Company	Holdings	Fleet
BET Omnibus Services Ltd (BETO)		
Aldershot & District	BETO, SR	291
East Kent	BETO, SR	544
East Midland	BETO, LMS, LNER	159
East Yorkshire	BETO, LNER	216
Maidstone & District (M&D)	BETO, SR	551
Chatham & District	M&D	50
North Western	BETO, LMS, LNER	552
Ribble	BETO, LMS	1,055
Standerwick	Ribble	92
Southdown	BETO, SR	734
Trent	BETO, LMS, LNER	365
Yorkshire Traction	BETO, LMS, LNER + others	287
BET		
City of Oxford	OTT, GWR	185
Devon General	NEC, GWR, SR	240
Hebble	BET, LMS, LNER	71
Mexborough & Swinton	NEC	36
Midland Red (BMMO)	BDIT, LMS, GWR, BETO	1,458
Stratford Blue	BMMO	21
Northern General (NGT)	BET, LNER	445
Sunderland District	NGT	89
Tynemouth & District	NGT + others	47
Tyneside	NGT	19
Wakefields	NGT	15
Potteries	BET	266
Rhondda	BET, NEC	137
South Wales	BET + others	322
Western Welsh	BET, GWR, NEC, BDIT	482
Yorkshire Woollen	BET, LMS, LNER	286

BDIT: Birmingham & District Investment Trust (owned by BET and BETO)
NEC: National Electric Construction Co (owned by BET)
OTT: Oxford Transport Trust (owned by NEC)

North Western was one of the casualties following the creation of the first passenger transport authorities in the early days of the National Bus Company. No 945 (VDB 945) is a 1963 AEC Reliance 2U3RA with BET-style Willowbrook 51-seat dual-purpose body, seen in Buxton on service to Manchester. The 'LMS' in the destination was strictly anachronistic, but was perhaps still familiar enough to inform passengers where they would be dropped in Manchester. *Policy Transport Photographs*

Slightly out on a limb, East Yorkshire was famous for its distinctive Beverley Bar-roofed double-deckers, shaped to allow normal-height buses to pass through the (nominally 10ft 9in) gothic archway in Beverley. No 488 (JAT 456), on layover at Hull in 1963, is a 1948 Leyland Titan PD1A with 54-seat Roe bodywork. *G. W. Dickson*

Some BET companies pursued individual vehicle policies in the 1930s, like Northern General, which built and operated 67 side-engined single-deckers. There were buses and coaches, and most were three-axle SE6 types, like No 727 (CN 7430), seen in 1950 on coach touring duties in Edinburgh.
A. T. Smith

During World War 2, BET companies, like all other British operators, could buy only a restricted number of new buses. Two 'unfrozen' AEC Regents with Northern Coachbuilders 55-seat lowbridge bodies are seen in 1942 before delivery to Western Welsh.
Ian Allan Library

Early postwar buses often bore more than a passing resemblance to their prewar brethren. Wakefields, one of the smaller Northern General Group companies, No W141 (FT 5711), a 1947 AEC Regent II with Weymann 56-seat body, is seen at Newcastle's Haymarket bus station when new.
Ian Allan Library

The 1942 agreement meant that virtually the entire map of England and Wales was covered by the areas of BET and Tilling companies. BET's strongholds, from north to south, were the concentrated area around Tyneside where Northern General operated, a swathe of country from the Lake District down through the northwest, Yorkshire, and the Midlands to South Wales and Oxford, another concentration in southeast England, and the isolated outpost of Devon General. Tilling, on the other hand, had companies in Cumberland, a substantial part of northeast England, West Yorkshire, Cheshire and North Wales, Lincolnshire and East Anglia, and south central England including the Isle of Wight. BET, largely because of its tramway roots, had landed the bus companies in the more populated and industrial parts of England and Wales, while Tilling seemed to have ended up with routes serving wide open stretches of countryside, leavened by more intensive services in areas like West Yorkshire and Essex, and urban networks like Bristol and Norwich.

The newly-reorganised BET Group struggled on through the war, coping with the unprecedented demand for public transport in many areas, without the benefit of a regular infusion of new buses. Older buses were retained and further service was coaxed out of them, while new deliveries, such as they were, helped to keep things moving. Some areas suffered particularly badly from war damage, with the East Kent company directly in the firing line of German bombers and guided rockets.

Restrictions on private motoring, still out of reach to a vast proportion of the population, and a desire to travel, meant that demand for public transport in the austere postwar years reached an all-time high, and operators worked hard to satisfy this. But costs were rising all around. At the annual meeting of the Aldershot & District company in 1948 it was revealed that a new double-deck bus which had cost £1,700 before the war was now costing £4,000. The resiting of factories out of urban centres to new out-of-town locations caused extra burdens for

New double-deckers were a source of local pride once these started flowing through after the war. Maidstone & District No DH248 (JKM 105), a 1947 AEC Regent III with Weymann 54-seat bodywork, is attracting attention in Tunbridge Wells. The Regent III was a sophisticated chassis, though the bodywork dated from 1942 (it had previously been used to rebody an older Regent) and is little changed visually from that on the 1939 Leyland Titan TD5 behind. *Ian Allan Library*

bus operators, who had to provide services against the normal traffic flow.

And there was the burden of tax on bus fuel, which meant that bus operators had to raise fares — often for the first time since 1939. BET was proud of the fact that bus fares had been pegged during the 1940s, but the ever-rising fuel tax bill (it rose nearly 300% between 1946 and 1955) forced fare increases. All of this was balanced by BET's constant drive for economies, and the growth in passenger numbers. In 1938 BET buses had carried 1,481 million passengers; in 1948 this figure had risen to 2,094 million; by 1955 it had risen to 2,328 million.
But just as things were beginning to settle down, and the flow of new buses was easing the load, a further danger appeared on BET's horizon — the spectre of nationalisation.

With the acquisition of the
National Electric
Construction Group in the
1930s, several other
companies passed into BET
control. These included
Devon General, whose
No 732 (PDV 732), a 1954
AEC Regent III 9613S (with
Birmingham-style tin front)
with Metro-Cammell Orion
58-seat bodywork, is seen in
Exeter in 1963. *A. J. Douglas/
Photobus*

Another ex-NEC company
which passed into the BET
net was Western Welsh,
whose No 416 (FUH 416) is
seen in June 1963 sweeping
into Bridgend bus station. It
is a 1951 Leyland Royal
Tiger PSU1/13 with
Weymann 44-seat body.
Similarly-bodied buses on
lighter Leyland Tiger Cub
chassis would feature in the
Western Welsh fleet for many
years. *P. R. Wallis*

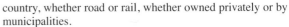

▼ 2. The Fight Against Nationalisation

The BET Group did not mince words in its contempt for state ownership. In *The Sixth Decade*, the second part of an ongoing official history of the BET Group, Roger Fulford wrote: 'The threat to BET was obvious and imminent. If the nationalisation of the electricity and gas undertakings might be compared with the loss of a limb, the provisions of the Transport Bill, so far ►► as they affected the bus interests of BET, were a clear indication that there was now no obstacle between the Company and the mortuary chamber'. The Bill, published late in 1946, included the Labour Government's plans for the nationalisation of the railways and long-distance road haulage, but contained the provision that the British Transport Commission (BTC) could prepare a scheme for the co-ordination of all passenger transport services in any area of the country, whether road or rail, whether owned privately or by municipalities.

The Group was worried about the threat of compulsory nationalisation, and its effects on a group which was torn between the ideals of public service and the need to return a handsome profit to its shareholders. But BET was already an unwilling partner in state ownership, as the newly formed British Railways in January 1948 automatically possessed something like a half-share in the BET, Tilling and SMT groups through the investments in the late 1920s by the four main-line companies. Following the shock Labour election win in 1945 railway nationalisation was not unexpected, but the decision by Tilling in September 1948 to sell its bus interests to the BTC was not what the BET directors wanted to hear. The consequences of the Tilling decision, according to Roger Fulford in *The Sixth Decade*, 'were so nearly mortal to the maintenance of free enterprise in the industry that the decision could not be passed in silence'. He continues: 'Certainly the Government had dangled a tempting bait before Tillings, for the terms of compensation were such that they must have made some of the pioneer theorists of socialism writhe in their graves. The gross amount paid by the Government to Tillings was £24,800,000 based on three main categories of imbursement. First, there was a payment for the loss of business based on the net annual profits; secondly, a payment for the real property acquired; and, thirdly, payment for the vehicles.'

The implication is that the generous payment to Tillings was a bait for others and certainly the SMT Group chose to follow Tilling into state ownership shortly afterwards. But BET stiffened its resolve and pledged to fight nationalisation to the last wheel. As BET Deputy Chairman and Managing Director, J. Spencer Wills said at the Group's jubilee dinner at London's Savoy Hotel on 29 October 1946: 'You can be sure of one thing; if we do go down it will be with our flag flying!'

There was pressure on BET to sell out, and the stock market certainly expected this for BET's value shot up in the wake of the Tilling sale. There was external pressure on BET Chairman, H. C. Drayton, to sell, but he held out obstinately and a year later was able to tell his shareholders that they had benefited from the board's decision not to sell because the group was now making a larger profit than the amount it would have received as interest on the purchase price.

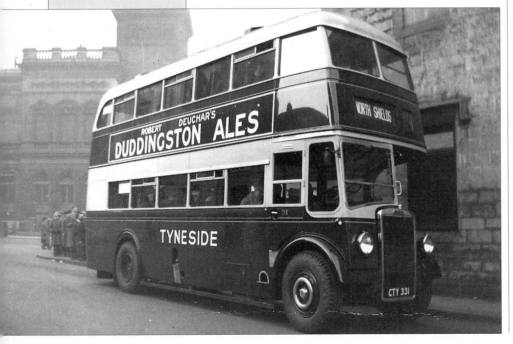

BET at least had the freedom to decide not to sell to BTC, but a new danger was looming that could have had a serious effect on the prosperity of BET. Rather as much of the British road haulage industry had been placed under the control of British Road Services, there were plans for area schemes that might do the same for bus operators on a regional basis.

The first area scheme was to be the Northern Passenger Road Transport Board, which would cover all of Northumberland and County Durham and a substantial chunk of North Yorkshire. In this area were over 4,000 buses and coaches operated by Tilling's United Auto company, municipalities at Darlington, Hartlepool, Middlesbrough, Newcastle, South Shields, Stockton, Sunderland, Teesside and West Hartlepool, and a large number of independents of all sizes. And there was BET's Northern General group, serving a concentrated but highly profitable network north and south of the Tyne and south into County Durham. Although the Act did not appear to nationalise road passenger transport, BET took the view that, provided that schemes could be prepared in which all forms of passenger transport in a specified area were to be co-ordinated, compulsory purchase was a distinct possibility. Compulsory purchase of Northern would rob BET of a valuable asset, and would presumably have been the first of a string of boards that would ultimately cover all of Britain. Certainly there were others proposed for East Anglia and southwest England, which would have been less contentious for BET, but any moves into BET heartlands like southeast or northwest England, Yorkshire or South Wales would have been fatal blows.

BET mounted a strong opposition to the plans. Northern General group buses wore anti-nationalisation posters with slogans like 'Is "nationalisation" of your journey really necessary', 'This bus is not nationalised — but without your help it may soon be', and 'Don't let nationalisation "take you for a ride". You would find it very expensive'. It is interesting to remember that half of the Northern group was actually owned by the BTC.

The area schemes never got off the ground. There was much prevaricating and Labour's reduced majority in 1950 and the Conservative victory of 1951 consigned the area schemes to the dustbin. It is interesting to speculate whether these schemes would have been necessary if BET had followed Tilling into state ownership. Although in opposition the Conservatives had pledged to return nationalised transport

The Northern General Group's lucrative service network in northeast England would have been at risk if the Government's proposed Northern Passenger Road Transport Board had gone ahead. Sunderland District No 293 (YPT 293), a 1958 Leyland Titan PD3/4 with Burlingham 73-seat body (though with rebuilt MCW Orion-style upper deck) leaves Sunderland bus station in 1971. *Policy Transport Photographs*

Sunderland District tried this lighter aquamarine blue in the 1960s, as worn here by No 317 (2517 PT), a 1961 Leyland Tiger Cub PSUC1/2 with BET-style Alexander 41-seat body, seen in July 1963. *R. L. Wilson*

Although East Anglia and southwest England were put forward as other passenger boards, if political power at Westminster had not changed there would surely have been more, affecting BET's most profitable companies. With BET's strong grip on South Wales through its Western Welsh and South Wales Transport companies, any moves in this area would have been firmly resisted. Western Welsh No 335 (XUH 335), a 1962 Leyland Atlantean PDR1/1 with Weymann semi-lowbridge 70-seat body (complete with some serious denting on the front panelling), is seen at Bridgend bus station in June 1963. *P. R. Wallis*

undertakings to their previous owners, the 1953 Transport Act merely gave the Government the power to direct BTC to divest itself of the controlling interest in bus companies, a power that was never exercised.

BET's interest in tramways ceased in 1951 with the closure of the Gateshead system, although the Swansea & Mumbles light railway remained; it passed into the control of the South Wales company and operated until it was replaced by buses in 1960.

In many ways this marked the end of the group's original *raison d'être*, but now BET was not only a substantial bus operator in England and Wales, it was also exercising its entrepreneurial skills by expanding into transport overseas, and into totally new businesses. This must in some way have been a reaction to the threat of nationalisation that hung over its bus interests, but BET was always on the look-out for a good investment. In 1955, buses were still responsible for the bulk of the group's income — £47,992,897 — with Rediffusion adding £8,965,099 and laundry companies £3,052,867.

BET had bought a substantial interest in Rediffusion, relaying radio and television signals, in 1947, and in 1955 formed, with Associated Newspapers, the Associated

◀◀ Rebodying of sturdy prewar and wartime chassis was a popular option for many operators, and North Western embarked on a substantial rebodying programme. In Manchester Piccadilly in May 1952 are two buses rebodied by Willowbrook — utility Guy Arab No 24 (BJA 109) and a prewar Bristol K5G in the background. *G. H. F. Atkins*

◀◀ Some interesting rebuilds were undertaken by operators in the 1950s — like this 1948 Guy Arab III with Northern Counties body (No H298, JVT 609), rebuilt in 1957 to forward-entrance 57-seat layout, apparently to gain experience of this entrance type, in anticipation of new buses on order. *Ian Allan Library*

◀◀ North Western was a keen Bristol customer until the sale of Tilling to the British Transport Commission in 1948 meant that Bristol chassis could only be sold to state-owned companies. No 305 (DDB 305), a 1950 Bristol L5G, ordered before the restrictions applied, with Weymann 35-seat body, is seen at Buxton. *G. H. F. Atkins*

◀ Eastern Coach Works bodies were also restricted to state-owned companies from 1948, but not before Ribble had sent a number of prewar Leyland chassis to ECW at Lowestoft for rebodying. At Liverpool in July 1959 is No 1792 (RN 8176), a 1938 Leyland Titan TD5 with 1948 ECW lowbridge 53-seat body. *G. Mead*

Rediffusion company, providing commercial television programmes for London on Mondays to Fridays. By the 1970s this side of BET's activities was contributing over 35% of the group's profits.

From the 1930s BET had been involved in laundries, and eventually its laundry interests were placed under Advance Laundries, providing a wide range of linen and towel hire and laundering services. In the 1950s BET was also involved with plant hire and road haulage, and had bus-operating interests in Jamaica and Africa. By the 1970s, without any UK bus interests, BET was a multi-faceted organisation, with the United Transport Company controlling its subsidiaries (mostly freight companies, but with bus operations in Kenya, Malawi, Rhodesia and South Africa). Many years later some of Stagecoach's first overseas forays followed the acquisition of United Transport bus operations in Kenya and Malawi.

Northern General Group buses in their various liveries and fleetnames served a compact area around Tyneside and County Durham. No 2341 (GCN 841G) is a 1969 Leyland Panther PSUR1A/1R with Marshall Camair 48-seat two-door body, ordered under BET ownership, but delivered in NBC days. *Policy Transport Photographs*

Ribble's vast territory stretched down into the network of towns to the north of Manchester, as well as into Manchester itself. At Bolton bus station in 1969, 1955 Leyland Titan PD2/12 No 1444 (JCK 519) with 61-seat Burlingham body awaits departure time on the Chorley service. Behind it are two of Ribble's large fleet of Marshall-bodied Leyland Leopards, bought in the 1960s. *P. Eckersley/Photobus*

The early underfloor-engined models were snapped up by BET companies, as they offered maximum capacity within the dimensions of the time —up to 45 seats. Yorkshire Woollen No 692 (HD 8546) is an example of the relatively rare home-market Leyland/MCW Olympic HR44 integral bus, a 44-seater, seen at Mill Street garage, Dewsbury. *Ian Allan Library*

Beadle was heavily involved in vehicle reconstruction in the postwar period, using parts from prewar AECs and Leylands to create ostensibly new semi-chassisless buses and coaches. East Kent GFN 265 is a 1952 35-seater based on Leyland Titan TD5 components, one of 30 for this fleet. *Ian Allan Library*

Ribble surprised many, including Leyland, by buying Beadle-bodied Sentinel STC4 underfloor-engined buses in 1949. No 283 (CRN 216) is seen in Carlisle in 1953. A further batch of Sentinels was bought in 1951, but Ribble soon reverted to Leylands. *A. M. Wright*

EAST KENT

GFN 265

In 1951 East Yorkshire bought 16 of these stylish Leyland Titan PD2/12s with full-fronted Roe bodies for longer-distance services. At Hull in 1963 is No 568 (MKH 77). Note the characteristic inward-sloping Beverley Bar roof. *G. W. Dickson*

The Hebble company traditionally maintained a good front-line coach fleet. No 17 (JHD 830) is a 1963 Leyland Leopard PSU3/1R with Plaxton's mould-breaking Panorama body, seen in 1972. *R. L. Wilson*

County Motors (Lepton) Ltd was jointly owned by Yorkshire Traction and Yorkshire Woollen and the independent West Riding company. This 1949 Leyland Tiger PS1 with BET-style Brush bodywork (No 83, EVH 211), seen in 1960, was one of many similar buses supplied to BET Group fleets in the early postwar years. *Arnold Richardson/Photobus*

3. The BET Group Companies

The 1942 reorganisation had given BET a useful portfolio of profitable bus companies, and this is the time to look at these in more detail, starting in the north.

Northern General Transport Co Ltd

Formed in 1913 to consolidate BET's bus interests in Tyneside and the northern part of County Durham, Gateshead-based Northern General became the parent for a number of other local companies which were already in the BET Group or which were subsequently acquired. Some retained their separate identities for many years, while others were absorbed into the local companies. Gateshead & District, Tynemouth & District, Tyneside Tramways & Tramroads, Wakefields, and Sunderland District were familiar names on Northern Group buses in their distinctive liveries for many years.

The Northern Group companies mainly operated in the area south of Newcastle, down into the northern part of County Durham. Northern's Tilling Group neighbour, United Auto, had a substantial area, from Northumberland to North Yorkshire, and there were operating agreements in the many areas their paths crossed. Important Northern bus services out of Newcastle were to Bishop Auckland, Crook, Darlington, Middlesbrough and West Hartlepool, and from Sunderland to Bishop Auckland and Consett.

Northern developed an extensive day and extended tour programme, ran seasonal express services from the northeast to Blackpool and the Lake District, and participated in the Yorkshire Services pool with other BET and Tilling Group companies.

Northern had individual ideas about vehicle design, and in an area peppered with low railway bridges sought ways of getting maximum capacity in single-deck buses. Its side-engined SE6 45-seaters and short-bonnet 39-seat AEC Regals helped in the 1930s and 1940s, and it was an enthusiastic customer for high-capacity underfloor-engined single-deckers from the 1950s.

In the postwar years it favoured AEC, Guy and Leyland buses, moving quickly on to higher-capacity double-deckers when these became available in the late 1950s — Northern built up a substantial fleet of Leyland Atlanteans and Daimler Fleetlines — and 36ft 53-seat AEC Reliances and Leyland Leopards. It surprised many when it bought 50 AEC/Park Royal forward-entrance Routemasters in 1964-5, the only RMs supplied new to an operator outside London. Non-standard single-deckers late in BET days were Leyland Panthers with two-door Marshall bodies.

Ribble Motor Services Ltd

The Ribble company was registered in June 1919 and the following April it absorbed the Preston branch of BAT. Through acquisition and natural growth it grew to cover a vast part of northwest England, from Carlisle to Manchester and Liverpool. In 1928 Ribble became a T&BAT subsidiary, and by 1930 the fleet included well over 650 buses; a decade later the fleet topped the 1,000 mark. From 1929 the LMS railway

company held 50% of the shares. The Blackpool coaching firm of W. C. Standerwick was acquired in 1932 and the name survived as a Ribble subsidiary until 1973. Scout of Preston was bought in 1961 and operated as a separate subsidiary until 1968.

Ribble's massive operating area included a full mix of services, from intensive urban to deeply rural. Its main bus services included Burnley-Bolton, Blackburn-Wigan, Warrington-Southport, Kendal-Keswick, Penrith-Keswick and Southport-Liverpool, and a substantial network of limited-stop and express services, many linking the industrial northwest with Blackpool and the Lake District. Ribble, with its subsidiaries Standerwick and Scout, operated long-distance services from towns and cities throughout Ribble's operating area to Birmingham and London.

Inevitably, perhaps, locally-built Leylands were favoured, and examples of most Leyland models were operated. Daimler and Guy supplied chassis to Ribble during the war, and Sentinel temporarily broke Leyland's monopoly in 1949-51, but otherwise the business went to Leyland. Significant vehicles included the different generations of double-deck coach built on Leyland Titan PD1 and PD2 chassis (the 'White

Ladies'), and the Leyland Atlanteans with MCW bodywork (the 'Gay Hostesses'). In its final days under BET, Ribble, after sampling Leyland's Panther, turned to the Bristol RELL chassis, admittedly with Leyland engines.

East Yorkshire Motor Services Ltd

This company was formed in 1926 by BAT to take over two operators in the Hull area, Lee & Beulah and Hull & District. In 1928 it became a T&BAT company, and the following year LNER acquired an equal share in the company. A co-ordination scheme with Hull Corporation came into effect in 1934.

Centred on Hull, East Yorkshire services radiated to the east coast, to the north and west to Selby and York. Its main services were between Hull and Goole, Leeds, Scarborough and Selby, and more locally to Aldbrough, Hornsea and Withernsea. A member of the Yorkshire Services pool, it also operated a Hull-Newcastle service and a seasonal Hull-Blackpool service.

Leyland-bodied Titan PD2s
like this one were familiar in
many BET fleets in the
postwar years. Yorkshire
Traction No 929 (DHE 567)
is a 1951 lowbridge PD2/12
with 53-seat body, seen in
May 1959. *Roger Holmes*

To lengthen the lives of early
postwar Leyland Tiger PS2
chassis, Yorkshire Woollen
had a number of these rebuilt
and rebodied as forward-
entrance double-deckers in
the 1960s. This is No 51
(HD 8554), a 1950 chassis
with 1963 Roe 63-seat body.
H. J. Black

A largely Leyland fleet was joined by AEC double-deckers from the 1950s —Regent Vs, Bridgemasters and Renowns. A high proportion of the double-deck fleet has been built with domed roofs to operate safely through the Gothic Beverley Bar.

Hebble Motor Services Ltd

This small BET company based in Halifax was formed in 1924 to operate between Halifax and Brighouse and Bingley, and soon expanded to main centres like Bradford and Leeds. The LMS and LNER railway companies bought Hebble in 1929 and set up the Halifax Joint Omnibus Committee with Halifax Corporation. BET bought a 50% share of the company in 1932 and operations concentrated on the Halifax and Bradford areas.

Main Hebble services operated between Halifax and Bradford, Bradford and Huddersfield, Leeds and Burnley, Bradford and Bingley and Leeds and Rochdale. Hebble was a member of the Yorkshire-Blackpool pool of services (with Ribble, West Yorkshire, Yorkshire Traction and Yorkshire

County Motors (Lepton) Ltd

This unusual company was jointly owned by three area companies — BET's Yorkshire Traction, Yorkshire Woollen subsidiaries, and the independent West Riding company. County served the area to the east of Huddersfield bounded by Dewsbury, Wakefield and Barnsley. Its small fleet reflected the purchases of its owners, so there were BET-style buses as well as two West Riding-inspired Guy Wulfrunians.

Yorkshire Woollen District Transport Co Ltd

Originally set up by BET as a tramway company in 1903, motorbuses first appeared in 1913 and replaced the trams by 1934. The LMS and LNER bought a half share in the company in 1929, which remained in BET, rather than T&BAT, control.

The buses of Dewsbury-based Yorkshire Woollen, which carried the fleetname 'Yorkshire', operated in an area north to Bradford and Leeds, west to Halifax, south to Huddersfield and east to Wakefield. Its main routes linked Dewsbury with Leeds, Bradford and Huddersfield; Leeds with Huddersfield and with Bradford. A member of the Yorkshire-Blackpool pool of operators, Yorkshire Woollen also ran a seasonal long-distance service linking Huddersfield and Dewsbury with Scarborough and Bridlington.

The fleet was typically BET, with AECs and Leylands of various types. Unusual purchases were Beadle-Commer coaches and Leyland-Albion Lowlanders with Weymann bodies. Daimler Fleetlines were bought latterly. Yorkshire Woollen had a number of Leyland Tiger single-deckers rebodied in the 1950s and 1960s as double-deckers.

Yorkshire Traction Co Ltd

Universally known as 'Tracky', Barnsley-based Yorkshire Traction dates back to 1902 and the BET's Barnsley & District Electric Traction company. Motorbuses started in 1913, and the Yorkshire Traction title was adopted in 1928. The LMS and LNER bought a substantial share in the company in 1929.

Centred on Barnsley, Tracky's area radiated out to Doncaster, Huddersfield and Pontefract. The main services were to Doncaster, by several routes, to Huddersfield, Pontefract, Rotherham and Sheffield. The company was part of the Yorkshire-Blackpool pool, and operated seasonal services from its area to Bridlington, Cleethorpes, Filey, Scarborough and Skegness.

Another strongly Leyland fleet, Tracky operated examples of most models and rebuilt older Leyland Tiger single-deckers and had them rebodied as double-deckers in the 1950s and 1960s.

Yorkshire Woollen used the fleetname 'Yorkshire' on its buses. This is No 501 (HD 7424), a 1943 Guy Arab II with 1954-built 56-seat Roe body, seen leaving Dewsbury bus station in 1963.
C. B. Golding

Mexborough & Swinton often acquired buses from other BET fleets. This is No 25 (KUF 704), a 1951 ex-Southdown Leyland Titan PD2/12 with Leyland 58-seat bodywork seen in Rotherham in 1968. *Roy Marshall/ Photobus*

North Western pursued a rather individual vehicle-buying policy, and in the 1960s bought lowheight AEC and Dennis double-deckers, as well as Daimler Fleetlines. No 978 (VDB 978) is a 1963 AEC Renown 3B3RA with Park Royal 74-seat body seen in Northwich bus station in 1972. *Policy Transport Photographs*

The early semi-lowbridge Leyland Atlanteans were popular with BET companies requiring maximum capacity and lowbridge bodies. East Midland No D135 (135 BRR), with 73-seat Weymann body, is seen at Mansfield in May 1963. *R. L. Wilson*

Mexborough & Swinton Traction Co Ltd

The National Electric Construction company set up Mexborough & Swinton as a tramway company and in 1907 started operations in the Rawmarsh, Swinton, Mexborough and Rotherham areas of Yorkshire. The company bought trolleybuses from 1915 and motorbuses from 1922, and in 1931 passed to BET with the NEC group. The trams were abandoned in 1929 and the trolleybuses took over the main route into Rotherham and another route linking Mexborough, Manvers Main Colliery, Conisborough and Swinton. The last M&S trolleybus — indeed BET's last — operated in March 1961, being largely replaced by Leyland Atlanteans. The fleet was mainly composed of Leyland buses.

East Midland Motor Services Ltd

W. T. Underwood Ltd started services in Clowne, Derbyshire in 1920 and grew by expansion and acquisition during the 1920s, serving the Doncaster, Sheffield, Rotherham and Chesterfield areas. The company title was adopted in 1927 and it was bought by the LMS and LNER railway companies the following year. In 1930 BET bought a 51% share and East Midland became a T&BAT subsidiary. It continued to grow, often by acquiring local operators. East Midland had been under Tilling management until 1942, but in the T&BAT split-up that year it was placed under BET control.

Based in Chesterfield, East Midland covered a compact area between Doncaster in the north, Rotherham and

The forward-entrance 30ft-long double-decker bridged the gap between the more traditional rear-entrance double-deckers and rear-engined models like the Daimler Fleetline and Leyland Atlantean. Yorkshire Traction No 1225 (XHE 225) is a 1962 Leyland Titan PD3A/1 with 73-seat Northern Counties body, complete with sliding door. *Ian Allan Library*

Before adopting a more conventional red/cream livery, East Midland buses were painted in this distinctive ochre/brown/cream style. No 325 (ORR 325), a 1954 Leyland Tiger Cub PSUC1/1 with 44-seat Saro body, is seen at Chesterfield in April 1954. *G. H. F. Atkins*

The Potteries company operated a mixed fleet, a result of its own slightly quirky buying policy and vehicles taken over with acquired local businesses. No SN415 (NEH 408) is an AEC Regal III with 35-seat Lawton body, acquired with the business of Stoke-on-Trent Motors Ltd in 1952 and seen in 1962.
Arnold Richardson/Photobus

Trent favoured locally-built Willowbrook bodies, as on No 140 (HRC 140), a 1955 Leyland Tiger Cub PSUC1/1 41-seat dual-purpose vehicle seen in 1963.
A. J. Douglas/Photobus

The giant Midland Red company comprised a number of fairly distinct networks, and in later years these would form the basis of the new smaller units when the company was split up. At Leicester bus station in 1964 is No 5329 (6329 HA), a 1963 BMMO-built D9 with 72-seat body. *R. G. Funnell*

An early 36ft-long coach, looking every inch of its length with its multi-windowed Alexander 49-seat body. No 909 (VDB 909) is a Leyland Leopard PSU3/1R, new in 1962. The body is a development of the style built for BET on shorter chassis, and was the forerunner of the famous Y type.
Ian Allan Library

Sheffield in the west, Mansfield in the south and Retford in the east.

Principal bus services ran between Chesterfield and Retford, Doncaster, Mansfield, Matlock Bath and Sheffield; Retford to Doncaster and Mansfield; and Worksop to Doncaster and Rotherham. Seasonal express services ran between Chesterfield and Skegness, Cleethorpes and Blackpool, and East Midland was a partner in the Yorkshire Services.

Leylands were favoured, and many different types were operated. Unusual purchases were Leyland-Albion Lowlanders, AEC Swifts and, in 1967-8, ECW-bodied Bristol RELLs.

North Western Road Car Co Ltd

BAT had started operating in the Macclesfield area in 1913, and after World War 1 expanded into the Buxton and Stockport areas. In 1923 a new company, owned by Tilling and BAT, was set up to continue these operations, taking the North Western

name. The LMS and LNER bought a 50% stake in the company in 1930.

The fleet was a varied one, and the company favoured Tilling-Stevens and Bristol buses in the interwar years, returning to Bristols after World War 2. The choice of Bristols had been influenced by the pre-1942 control of North Western by Tilling, but, surprisingly, after the split-up that year the company was firmly in the BET camp.

After the Bristols North Western turned to Leylands and AECs, relieved by unusual batches of buses like Atkinson Alphas, Dennis Lolines and Bedford VALs; the Bedfords had special low-height Strachans bodies for operation under Dunham Woodhouses Bridge on the Bridgwater Canal. North Western's later double-deck policy was interesting: as well as the Lolines it bought AEC Renowns and Daimler Fleetlines. It returned to its roots when it bought Bristol RESLs in 1968.

Based in Stockport, North Western operated into Manchester, around its southern flanks, south to Buxton and Crewe, west to Warrington and east to Barnsley and Sheffield. Its main bus services linked Macclesfield with Crewe; Manchester with Blackpool, Buxton, Glossop, Hayfield and

Macclesfield; and Buxton with Derby and Sheffield. It operated express services out of Manchester to Derby, Llandudno, Bangor, Nottingham and Scarborough; and out of Oldham to Blackpool. It also participated in the Tyne-Tees-Mersey group of services and ran Manchester-London jointly with Midland Red.

Potteries Motor Traction Co Ltd

The Potteries Electric Traction company was set up by BET in 1898 when it acquired North Staffordshire Tramways. The trams only lasted until 1928 and the name was changed to Potteries Motor Traction (PMT) in 1933. Unusually, there was no railway interest in PMT. In the postwar years it grew by acquisition.

The Potteries fleet was a mixed one, and contained many vehicles acquired with local businesses. In addition to the standard BET AEC and Leyland types, PMT favoured Daimler double-deckers in the postwar years, and bought lightweight single-deckers including Albion Aberdonians and Beadle-Commer coaches. It bought Daimler Fleetlines and Leyland Atlanteans in the later BET years and was the first customer for Daimler's unsuccessful Roadliner single-deck model.

Based in Stoke-on-Trent, PMT served the immediate Potteries area, with interurban services to Manchester, Buxton, Derby and Birmingham. The main bus services ran between Hanley and Stafford, Congleton, Crewe; and between Newcastle-under-Lyme and Market Drayton. Express services operated between the Potteries towns and Manchester and Birmingham.

Trent Motor Traction Co Ltd

This company started up in 1913, jointly owned by BAT and Commercial Car Hirers. After World War 1 the company expanded, and in 1928 control passed to T&BAT. In 1929 the LMS and LNER bought a shareholding.

For years Trent bought Midland Red-built SOS vehicles, but in the mid-1930s moved to AECs and later to Daimlers and Leylands. In recent years the fleet was almost entirely AEC or Leyland, until the arrival of Daimler Fleetline double-deckers and, in the final days of BET ownership, typically Tilling ECW-bodied Bristol RESH dual-purpose vehicles.

A one-off Daimler double-decker for Potteries was H8900 (900 EVT), a 1958 CVD6-30 (with Daimler CD6 turbocharged engine) and 69-seat forward-entrance Northern Counties body. It was later fitted with a Leyland O.600 engine. *Ian Allan Library*

An early version of the famous BET-style body for 36ft single-deckers, with rounded rear end, built in 1963 by Willowbrook on Leyland Leopard PSU3/1R chassis for Trent —No 218 (218 CCH). *Ian Allan Library*

48

Although it was owned by Midland Red, Stratford Blue continued to buy other types of bus, notably Leylands. No 20 (TNX 454) is a 1956 Leyland Titan PD2/12 with 63-seat Willowbrook body, seen in 1971 at Stratford bus station. *Roy Marshall/Photobus*

Although Western Welsh built up a substantial fleet of Leylands, it also dual-sourced and bought AECs. No 707 (707 CUH), a 1963 AEC Regent V 2MD3RA with Northern Counties 65-seat forward-entrance body, is seen at Cardiff bus station in July 1963. *P. R. Wallis*

▲   Trent, based in Derby, operated services in all directions —
north to Matlock, Mansfield and Chesterfield, east to
Nottingham, south to Loughborough and Burton upon Trent,
and west to Uttoxeter. Principal services linked Derby with
Alfreton, Buxton, Nottingham, Swadlincote and Uttoxeter, and
Nottingham with Mansfield, Chesterfield, Doncaster and
Loughborough.

Trent had seasonal express coach services from
Derby/Nottingham to Yarmouth, Skegness and Cleethorpes,
and from other parts of its area to resorts around England.

Birmingham & Midland Motor Omnibus Co Ltd

The biggest of the BET bus companies was formed in 1905
following BET's acquisition of the Birmingham General
Omnibus company. Control of this company passed to
Birmingham & Midland Tramways, another BET company,
and BMMO experimented with buses until 1907, and there
was a five-year gap until the buses ran again. Further
acquisitions helped the BMMO empire to grow, and soon its

buses were covering a substantial part of the English
Midlands.

From the early 1920s BMMO built most of its own buses
and coaches, and supplied firms like Northern General and
Trent. The company pioneered many advanced design
features, like underfloor-engined buses, disc brakes, air
suspension and integral construction. It introduced underfloor-
engined single-deckers in quantity after World War 2, and
developed these over the years with improved specifications
and taking advantage of increases in vehicle dimensions.
There were also batches of bespoke double-deckers, AECs,
Daimlers, Guys and Leylands, to complement the BMMO-
built types. These, like BMMO-built single-deckers, included
advanced features like independent front suspension.

On the BET map, BMMO, better known to many by its
fleetname, Midland Red, covered a large part of the English
Midlands, stretching across to the Welsh border in the west.
Based in Birmingham, the company had several distinct areas
which were often large enough to be separate companies in
their own right — as was to happen in 1982.

The Birmingham area included frequent services from that
city to Bromsgrove, Stourbridge, Tamworth and
Wolverhampton and all parts of Midland Red's vast area,
many on a limited-stop basis, as well as local services in the
greater Birmingham area. The Worcester area included
services from Bewdley, Evesham, Malvern and Stourport to
Birmingham, and from Worcester to Hereford and Stourbridge.
The Shrewsbury area included services from Bridgnorth and
Ludlow to Birmingham, and from Shrewsbury to Edgmond
and Market Drayton. The Stafford area included services to
Birmingham from Burton, Cannock and Stafford, and between
Stafford and Cannock, and Dudley and Lichfield. The
Leicester area included services from Leicester and
Nottingham to Birmingham, and between Leicester and Ashby,
Coalville, Coventry and Loughborough. The Leamington area
included services linking Coventry and Stratford with
Birmingham, and services between Coventry and Lichfield,
Coventry and Leicester, and Rugby and Daventry.

Midland Red was one of the founding members of
Associated Motorways, operating an intensive network of
services in the Midlands, southwest England, South Wales and
the West Country. Under its own name, Midland Red operated
services from the Midlands to London, and there was the
network of limited-stop interurban services linking centres in

its own operating area with points beyond. And there were the summer services linking the Midlands with seaside resorts on the east and west coasts.

Stratford-upon-Avon Blue Motors Ltd

Stratford Blue was started by local residents in 1927, competing with the expanding Midland Red. In 1929 the business passed to the Balfour Beatty Group, and in 1935 it was bought by Midland Red, which maintained it as a separate business. Interestingly, very few BMMO-built buses were operated, and the company latterly concentrated on Leyland single-deck and double-deck models.

City of Oxford Motor Services Ltd

Motorbus operation by the City of Oxford tramways company, an NEC company, began in 1913, the familiar company name

being adopted in 1921. When NEC was taken over in 1931, control of City of Oxford passed to BET. GWR bought a 50% interest in 1931.

City of Oxford operated in a compact area, but through its links with other territorial operators offered connections to a substantial part of southern England. The company's buses linked with United Counties at Buckingham and Aylesbury; London Transport at Aylesbury and High Wycombe; Thames Valley at Aylesbury, High Wycombe, Henley-on-Thames and Reading; Aldershot & District at Reading; Wilts & Dorset at Newbury; Bristol Tramways at Lechlade; and Midland Red at Banbury.

City of Oxford's main longer-distance routes linked Oxford with Aylesbury, Newbury, Reading and Swindon, with a network of city services in Oxford itself.

Traditionally an AEC fleet, City of Oxford operated Regals, Regents, Reliances, Swifts, Bridgemasters and Renowns, the only variety in later years being provided by Dennis Lolines (with AEC engines) and Daimler Fleetlines.

Western Welsh Omnibus Co Ltd

South Wales Commercial Motors was formed in 1920, coming under NEC control in 1927. GWR acquired a shareholding in 1929 when the Western Welsh name was adopted. BET assumed control when it acquired the NEC business in 1931.

Based in Cardiff, Western Welsh covered a substantial part of South Wales, with intensive services in Cardiff and the valleys, and more rural services in the Carmarthen, St Davids, Cardigan and Aberaeron areas of West Wales. Principal services included links between Cardiff and Carmarthen, Ebbw Vale, Garndiffaith and Porthcawl; between Newport and Ebbw Vale and Tredegar; between Neath and Porthcawl; between Neath and Merthyr; and between Carmarthen and Cardigan. Seasonal express services ran between South Wales and Aberystwyth.

The fleet was a mix of AECs and Leylands, with a substantial fleet of Leyland Tiger Cubs built up over a number of years. Unusual purchases included AEC Bridgemasters and Albion Nimbuses.

▲ South Wales Transport Co Ltd

BET formed South Wales to provide feeder bus services to and from the termini of its Swansea trams, which were finally replaced by buses in 1937. There was no railway shareholding in South Wales. After electricity privatisation BET acquired the Llanelly & District company, whose trolleybuses were replaced by South Wales motorbuses in 1952. Another local ◄ BET bus company, J. James & Sons Ltd of Ammanford, was absorbed into the South Wales fleet in 1962.

Although its title suggested a wider coverage, the South Wales area was restricted to an arc around Swansea, reaching out to Carmarthen, Llandeilo, Brecon, Neath and Porthcawl, where it met the buses of its fellow BET company, Western Welsh. Principal bus services included Swansea town services; Swansea to Ystradgynlais, Llanelli, Margam and Porthcawl; and Llanelli to Carmarthen and Neath. The South Wales company was heavily involved in coach touring in Britain and overseas.

South Wales was another AEC-dominated BET fleet, with Regals, Regents, Reliances, Bridgemasters and Renowns, with only the Leylands inherited from James of Ammanford providing variety.

Rhondda Transport Co Ltd

Electric trams were introduced to the Rhondda area of South Wales in 1908 by an NEC company, Rhondda Tramways, which from 1920 also operated motorbuses. The tramway closed in 1934, and the company name was changed. BET assumed control when it bought out NEC in 1931.

The bus fleet in later years was comprised AEC double-deckers and Leyland single-deckers.

Aldershot & District Traction Co Ltd

The Aldershot & District company was formed by BAT in 1912 to take over an existing operator, and in 1930 the Southern Railway acquired a shareholding. From 1928 to 1942 it was a T&BAT company.

A&D, based at Aldershot, operated mainly in Surrey, reaching out to Berkshire, Hampshire and Sussex. Its main bus services were between Aldershot and Basingstoke, Camberley, Guildford, Midhurst, Petersfield, Reading, Winchester and Woking; and between Guildford and Camberley, Farnham, Haslemere, Hindhead, Petersfield and Woking.

A regular express service was provided between Farnham/Aldershot and London, and there were summer services linking with resorts on the south coast.

With Dennis based at Guildford, A&D favoured the local product, buying Dennis single- and double-deckers for many years. Only when Dennis stopped offering a single-deck chassis did the company turn to AEC, but Lance and then Loline double-deckers were bought right to the end of the company's separate existence.

East Kent Road Car Co Ltd

Many of the roots of BET's bus operations were in the East Kent company, formed in 1916 to bring together a number of operators in that area. East Kent became a T&BAT company in 1928 and in 1930 the Southern Railway acquired an interest.

Sitting in Aldershot & District's Guildford garage in June 1969 are two AEC Reliances —No 330 (SOU 438), a 1958 MU3RV example with Weymann 41-seat body, and No 420 (420 DHO), a 1961 2MU3RV with Park Royal 41-seat body. *Mike Barbour*

Following wartime experience with utility vehicles, East Kent became a good customer for Guy Arab double-deck chassis. FFN 380 (East Kent did not use fleet numbers), a 1951 Arab III with open-top Park Royal 56-seat body, parks up at London's Victoria Coach Station on 2 June 1965. A fair distance from its normal haunts on the Kent coast, its presence is explained by the fact that this was Derby Day, when all open-toppers were pressed into service. *Mike Barbour*

Aldershot & District chose normal-control Dennis Falcon P5s for its more rural routes. No 247 (LOU 75), new in 1954 with 30-seat Strachans body, is seen in Selborne in 1959. *Ian Allan Library*

East Kent was well placed to participate in the Europabus network, and coaches like this 1957 AEC Reliance with Beadle 37-seat body (MJG 286) were painted in a pale blue livery. *Ian Allan Library*

Maidstone & District acquired the Hastings Tramways Co in 1935, and the Hastings trolleybuses were finally withdrawn in 1959. No 20 (BDY 795), a 1940 AEC 661T with Park Royal 54-seat body, is seen in 1956. *Ian Allan Library*

Based in Canterbury, East Kent covered a wide area of Kent, bounded by the sea on three sides and fellow BET company, Maidstone & District, to the west.

East Kent's territory included the Channel ports of Dover and Folkestone, and this encouraged the company to pioneer continental coach tours in 1919, and it became heavily involved in contract work on behalf of airline and ferry companies, and the Europabus service network. Its main express services linked towns in the company area with London.

Dennises and Leylands were favoured for many years, but the company moved to Guy double-deckers in the postwar years, moving on to AECs in the late 1950s. Postwar single-deckers were built by Dennis and Leyland, and later by AEC.

Maidstone & District Motor Services Ltd

This company was registered in 1911 with backing from BAT, and grew after World War 1 to cover a wide area of West Kent. A T&BAT company from 1928, the Southern Railway acquired an interest in 1930 and it reverted to BET in 1942. The

Hastings Tramways Co was acquired in 1935, but was not fully absorbed until 1957. The Hastings trolleybuses were finally withdrawn in 1959, replaced by M&D Leyland Atlanteans.

Centred on Maidstone, M&D's area was bounded by water to the north and south, by East Kent on the east, and by London Transport and Southdown on the west. Its main bus services linked Maidstone with Faversham, Folkestone, Hastings and Sevenoaks; Chatham with Penhurst and Tunbridge Wells; Hastings with Eastbourne; Gravesend with Brighton and Sheerness; and Tunbridge Wells with East Grinstead.

M&D had regular coach services to London from Sheerness, Faversham and Gillingham, from Tenterden and Maidstone, and from Bexhill, Hastings and Rye.

The M&D fleet was more mixed than others, with Bristol single-deckers and double-deckers being bought in the postwar years, as well as AECs, Beadle-Commers, Commers, Daimlers, Dennises and Leylands.

Southdown Motor Services Ltd

The company was formed in 1915 to amalgamate three existing Sussex operators. BET was involved from the beginning and as Southdown grew in the 1920s, it became a T&BAT subsidiary in 1928, and the Southern Railway bought an interest in 1930. In 1942 Southdown reverted to BET control.

Southdown, based in Brighton, operated the length of the Sussex coast between Hastings and Fareham, stretching inland to Petersfield, Midhurst, Petworth, Horsham, East Grinstead, Tunbridge Wells and Hawkhurst, where its buses linked with those of other operators. Principal Southdown services were between Brighton and Arundel, Eastbourne, Gravesend, Horsham, Littlehampton, Southsea and Tunbridge Wells; between Southsea and Petersfield and Warsash; between Bognor and Horsham and Midhurst; and between Eastbourne and East Grinstead and Hastings.

The company was heavily involved in the coach traffic between the South Coast and London, with services from Bognor, Brighton, Chichester, Eastbourne, Gosport, Hayling Island, Lewes, Littlehampton, Portsmouth, Southsea and Worthing. Southdown was also involved in the South Coast Express Service with East Kent and Royal Blue, operating from Margate to Bournemouth, and serving Hastings,

Parked at Victoria Coach Station in 1968 beside a line of Midland Red motorway coaches, Southdown No 1151 (8151 CD) is a 1961 Leyland Tiger Cub PSUC1/2 with Weymann Fanfare 37-seat coach body. Weymann, first and foremost a service bus builder, produced coach models with varying degrees of success, and Southdown bought examples of this and the longer Castilian. *Arnold Richardson/Photobus*

Maidstone & District was one of a small number of BET fleets to flirt with the rear-engined Leyland Panther chassis. No 3064 (JKK 164E) is a 1967 PSUR/1R model with 53-seat Willowbrook body, seen in Maidstone in 1971. *C. Routh/Photobus*

Eastbourne, Brighton, Worthing, Portsmouth and Southampton.

Always closely associated with Leylands, Southdown bought other types, notably Guy Arabs during and after World War 2, Commer coaches and, right at the end before absorption into NBC, Bristol RESLs.

Devon General Omnibus & Touring Co Ltd

BET's rather isolated West Country fleet was created in 1919 and taken over by NEC's Torquay Tramways company three years later. The Great Western and Southern Railway companies bought an interest in 1929, and in 1931 control passed to BET with the acquisition of NEC.

Based in Exeter, Devon General's operating area was totally surrounded by the Western National/Southern National companies. Its principal bus services linked Exeter with Exmouth, Newton Abbot, Okehampton, Sidmouth and Tiverton; Newton Abbot with Buckfastleigh and Totnes; and Torquay with Newton Abbot and Teignmouth.

In an important coach touring area, Devon General's Grey Cars coach fleet provided a substantial programme of day tours.

Coaching Companies

BET also controlled a number of locally-based coaching companies that ran independently of the local BET bus companies. Starting in the north there were Sheffield United Tours Ltd, Black & White Motorways Ltd, Neath & Cardiff

In Exeter High Street in July 1963, with just a handful of Hillman and Ford cars around, is Devon General No 944 (944 HTT), a 1962 AEC Regent V with 59-seat Metro-Cammell Orion bodywork, complete with offside illuminated advertisement panel. *Roy Marshall/Photobus*

Operating express coach services between Cardiff and Swansea, Neath & Cardiff was one of BET's smaller companies. Reg No 3280 WB, a 1958 ex-Sheffield United Tours AEC Reliance MU3RV with Burlingham Seagull 41-seat body, is seen at Cardiff bus station in June 1968. *Policy Transport Photographs*

Luxury Coaches Ltd, Blue Cars Continental Coach Cruises Ltd, London Coastal Coaches Ltd, Red Line Continental Motorways Ltd, A. Timpson & Sons Ltd, and Greenslades Tours Ltd.

Sheffield United Tours was based on a company bought in 1935 by the East Midland, North Western and Yorkshire Traction bus companies, and SUT grew by acquisitions. It operated British and Continental tours, and operated a fleet that was latterly composed mainly of AEC Reliances with high-quality coach bodies, mainly by Plaxton.

Black & White, based at Cheltenham, started in 1928 running local tours but expanded by introducing coach services. Bristol Tramways, City of Oxford and Midland Red bought the company, which became an important component in the Associated Motorways grouping. Its coaches were always distinctive and well-specified, and included AEC, Bristol, Daimler and Guy types.

Neath & Cardiff's main operations were express coach services between Cardiff and Swansea. AEC and Guy

chassis were favoured.

Blue Cars and Red Line were BET's continental tours specialists, with luxury coaches often based on the Continent for this specialised work.

London Coastal Coaches started as a pool of coach operators running between London and the South Coast, and later developed Victoria Coach Station as a principal London terminal.

Timpson's started with horse-drawn coaches, moving on to motorcoaches, and regular services between London and the South Coast. The shares were bought during World War 2 by BET and Tilling. AECs were favoured for the main coach fleet, augmented by Commers and Fords.

Greenslades was set up in 1912, providing charabanc tours in Devon, and grew, operating coach tours and bus services. BET bought the business in 1953. In addition to local coach touring and private hire work, Greenslades operated extended tours in Britain and the Continent. AECs and Bedfords were favoured.

Sheffield United Tours received the very first Plaxton Panorama body in 1958, the aptly named 'Panorama Pioneer', on AEC Reliance chassis — No 286 (3286 WB). The Panorama introduced the concept of longer side windows to British coach bodies, and was to firmly establish Plaxton in the front rank of British coachbuilders. SUT went on to buy successive Panorama variants. *Ian Allan Library*

A brand-new Black & White Motorways AEC Reliance 2MU3RA with Harrington Grenadier 41-seat coach body, No 251 (AAD 251B) turns into the AEC works at Windmill Lane, Southall. The clean black/white livery suited the crisp lines of the Grenadier body. *Ian Allan Library*

The smart coaches of Black
& White were a familiar sight
running on Associated
Motorways services. No 272
(HDG 772D) is a 1966
Daimler Roadliner SRC6
with Plaxton Panorama
47-seat bodywork, seen in
Hereford bus station in July
1970. The Roadliner was
Daimler's unsuccessful rear-
engined single-deck model,
bought by Potteries in bus
form and Black & White in
coach form. *R. L. Wilson*

Northern General was the
only BET fleet — and indeed
the only fleet outside London
— to choose the advanced
AEC/Park Royal Routemaster
model. In 1964/5 it bought
50 forward-entrance 72-seat
Leyland-engined examples,
such as No 2095 (RCN 695),
seen in Sunderland in August
1969. *Policy Transport
Photographs*

4. The BET Group Fleet

The BET Group exercised a rather looser control on the fleet purchases of its subsidiaries than did the Tilling Group. Tilling, with Bristol chassis and ECW bodies built by fellow state-owned companies, had a good reason to favour the products of the Brislington and Lowestoft factories, buses and coaches which were, in any case, largely designed for them.

With rather more intensive services in industrial areas, the managers of BET companies had their own ideas about the ideal buses to serve them. They were given a fair amount of flexibility to buy the types of bus they wanted as long as the financial results were what the group was looking for. The odd disastrous batch of buses was not a problem as long as the company was successful overall.

It would be wrong to give the impression that there was no central influence on vehicle-buying. BET, with over 11,000 buses in 1952, was a significant customer, and the chassis and body manufacturers were only too aware of BET's spending power. Models were introduced with BET very much in mind as a major customer. Similarly, models may have been shelved, and certainly died, without BET support.

Analysis of BET's vehicle intake in the 1950s and 1960s suggests that the choice of chassis was fairly restricted, as BET took advantage of its size to negotiate good prices. There were BET-favoured bodybuilders too, and BET companies were sometimes able to stick with the products of one or two builders, while on other occasions they took what they could get.

With Bristol and ECW catering for the great majority of the Tilling Group's needs, and a proportion of the Scottish Group's needs, BET was an important customer for AEC and Leyland, with Daimler coming on stream with the Fleetline, and there were also isolated pockets where Atkinson, Dennis, Guy and Sentinel got a look in. For coaches, Bedford, Commer and Ford chassis were bought.

More bodybuilders figured in BET company orders, but some, like Beadle, Brush, Burlingham, East Lancs, Roe and Strachans never really broke through, and were often bought because of local connections. Alexander and Northern Counties managed to win BET business in the 1950s and 1960s, and Harrington and Saro enjoyed a limited success, but the main business was divided between Marshall, Metro-Cammell, Park Royal and Willowbrook. BET business was an essential part of the output of these bodybuilders, so when, following the sale of BET to THC and the creation of NBC, the integral Leyland National became the group's standard single-decker, it signalled the start of a potentially difficult period for them.

The BET Federation, previously the British Electrical Federation (BEF), the group's central servicing organisation, had been involved in the design and specification of single-deck bus bodies for the group's needs from the late 1920s. From the early 1930s a distinctive BEF style began to appear, built by bodybuilders like Brush (which was associated with BET), ECW, Roe and Weymann, usually on Leyland Tiger, though this style also appeared on AEC, Albion, Daimler, Dennis and Tilling-Stevens chassis. The design could be built in front-entrance or rear-entrance styles, and there were local variations. Other BET companies chose to develop their own quite different single-deck bus body styles, so there was no imposition of BET's will on all companies. The Federation design, though, offered an attractive, well thought-out, practical bus that suited others.

Federation designs went on Leyland to Coast Line (a small Scottish company, absorbed by SMT in 1936), East Midland, East Yorkshire, Lincolnshire, Sunderland District, Thames Valley (then under BET control, later Tilling), Western Welsh, Yorkshire Traction and Yorkshire Woollen.

Individual designs were favoured by Aldershot & District (on Dennis), City of Oxford (on AEC), Devon General (on AEC), East Kent (on Dennis and Leyland), Maidstone & District (mainly on Leyland), North Western (various chassis, under Tilling control until 1942), Northern General (on AEC and Leyland), Potteries (on Daimler and Leyland), Rhondda (on AEC), Ribble (on Leyland), South Wales (on AEC, Daimler, Dennis and Leyland), Southdown (on Leyland), Trent (on BMMO-built SOS), and Wilts & Dorset (then under BET control, later Tilling).

Midland Red, of course, went its own way with a succession of SOS models that were suited to its own needs, and found

Southdown resisted the rear-engined double-decker in BET days and built up a large fleet of Northern Counties-bodied Leyland Titan PD3s, the famous 'Queen Marys'. No 268 (BUF 268C), a 1965 Titan PD3/4 69-seater, is seen at Brighton's Pool Valley bus station in 1972. *Arnold Richardson/Photobus*

High capacity double-deckers were popular in the BET Group, which was also a major user of forward-entrance deckers after these became popular in the late 1950s. East Yorkshire No 750 (3750 RH) is a 1963 AEC/Park Royal Bridgemaster 2B3RA 72-seater, seen in Hull in 1970. Although a lowheight bus, EY also specified the Beverley Bar inward-tapering upper deck. The Leyland Leopard on the left is in the brighter blue. *Roy Marshall/Photobus*

Potteries, which had a reasonably-sized fleet of Daimler double-deckers, came unstuck when it opted for the Roadliner SRC6 model in the mid-1960s; this turned out to be a troublesome chassis. No S1081 (KVT 181E), with Marshall 50-seat body, is seen at Stoke garage in 1970. *Policy Transport Photographs*

ready customers at Northern General, until the mid-1930s, and
Trent, until 1940.

During World War 2, the BET companies, like every other
operator in Britain, took what vehicles were allocated by the
Ministry of War Transport, and after the war, although some
fleets managed to get hold of buses that matched their prewar
deliveries others took anything they could get their hands on.
BET Federation developed a postwar version of its single-deck
bus body and this, built by various bodybuilders, figured in
several fleets, while others specified their own styles — often
slightly updated versions of what had been built in the 1930s.

As a stopgap measure many operators turned to rebuilding
and rebodying wartime and prewar buses, and Beadle took this
a stage further with its programme of rebuilds, using AEC and
Leyland mechanical parts built into a new, fully-fronted bus or
coach. These were favoured by BET companies on the south
coast, like East Kent, Maidstone & District and Southdown,

and in Yorkshire. Later rebuilds involved early postwar
Leyland single-deckers which were rebuilt and rebodied by
Northern Counties and Roe as forward-entrance double-deckers
for Stratford Blue, Yorkshire Traction and Yorkshire Woollen.

With the type of operating areas of many of the BET fleets,
high-capacity buses were essential. Before the war, 32-5 seats
were the norm for single-deck buses, though Northern General
had developed a short-bonnet version of the AEC Regal with
seats for 38, and had built its own SE6 types with 45 seats.
Midland Red's own-build ON and SON types could also carry
38 seated passengers.

It was Midland Red that won the race to get underfloor-
engined single-deckers into production after the war. AEC and
Leyland had dabbled with underfloor-engined vehicles in the
late 1930s, and Leyland and BMMO had introduced
experimental rear-engined designs. In 1946 BMMO's S6
model went into production; this was an underfloor-engined

40-seater built to the then current maximum dimensions of 27ft 6in long and 7ft 6in wide. The major manufacturers rushed to get underfloor-engined models ready by 1949-50, by which time the maximum dimensions for single-deckers had increased to 30ft by 8ft. This allowed seats for 44-45 passengers, and the BET Group was a willing customer.

The first generation of underfloor-engined single-deckers were substantial vehicles, with heavy chassis and powerful engines. When bodied they weighed in around the 8-ton mark, and while they were rugged and powerful, they were very thirsty. In spite of this, the first generation chassis were snapped up by BET companies, mainly Leyland's Royal Tiger (and its integral sister, the Olympic), but also the AEC Regal IV. Ribble stirred things up at Leyland when it bought batches of underfloor-engined Sentinel buses, and if this was partly to spur Leyland into some action it seemed to work. After that, Ribble stuck firmly with Leyland.

Like other operators, BET was concerned that the new single-deckers were costly to operate, and was constantly badgering the manufacturers to produce lighter-weight and more economical buses. With one eye firmly focused on the balance-sheet, BET was looking for maximum capacity and minimum cost. The manufacturers responded in 1953-4 with the AEC Reliance and Leyland Tiger Cub, and BET was to be a major customer for both chassis.

There were in both BET 'AEC fleets' and 'Leyland fleets', as well as some that seemed happy to be a mix of both. So Reliances went to Aldershot & District, City of Oxford, Devon General, East Kent, Hebble, Maidstone & District, South Wales and Yorkshire Woollen, and Tiger Cubs went to East Yorkshire, Mexborough & Swinton, Rhondda, Ribble, Southdown, Stratford Blue and Yorkshire Traction. Most of the others were apparently content to take batches of both models.

A more conventional
Potteries Daimler, a 1956
CVG5 with 59-seat lowbridge
Northern Counties body,
No L6665 (XVT 665), at
Stoke garage in 1970.
*Policy Transport
Photographs*

Lightweight single-deckers,
offering maximum capacity
with performance and fuel
economy, were popular in
BET Group fleets. Yorkshire
Traction No 1018 (GHE 18),
a Leyland Tiger Cub
PSUC1/1 with 44-seat Saro
body, is seen in 1965.
R. G. Funnell

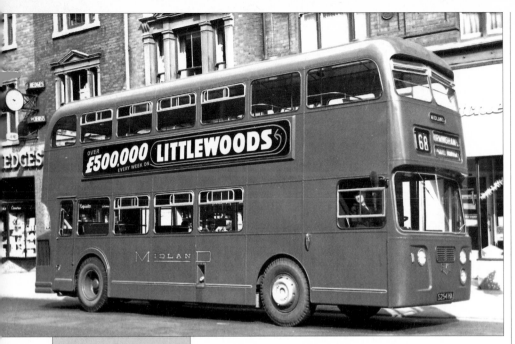

After a series of advanced BMMO-built double-deckers, Midland Red turned to Daimler for its rear-engined Fleetline model. No 5254 (5254 HA), with 77-seat Alexander body, is seen in 1963 in Birmingham. Midland Red classed these type DD11. *G. Mead*

Other underfloor-engined types were placed in service as well, though in much smaller quantities. Guy Arabs were bought by Aldershot & District and Northern General; Atkinson Alphas by North Western; Albion Aberdonians by East Yorkshire, North Western, Northern General and Potteries; Dennis Lancet UFs by Aldershot & District and East Kent; a Saro integral by Maidstone & District.

Bodywork was initially to the builder's designs, but during the 1950s a BET style was evolved; this was an efficient, rather square-styled design, that would pave the way for later styles. The first flush of lighter-weight underfloor-engined buses were largely bodied by Beadle, Burlingham, Saro, Weymann and Willowbrook, and the BET design was built by Alexander, Harrington, Marshall, Metro-Cammell, Park Royal and Willowbrook.

Double-deckers, too, had been going through a weight-saving phase, and while there were ultra-lightweight bodies like the MCW Orion on the market, BET appears to have imposed fewer restrictions when it came to double-deck buses,

so the range tended to be wider. AECs and Leylands were the most popular choices, inevitably, though East Kent, Potteries and Southdown also bought Guy Arabs and Aldershot & District, inevitably, bought Dennis double-deckers — but so, after the Loline was available, did City of Oxford and North Western. Potteries continued to favour Daimlers.

The relaxation that allowed 30ft by 8ft double-deckers from 1956 was welcomed by BET, as this allowed front-engined double-deckers to seat up to 74 passengers. Most fleets took the chance to move to forward entrances on double-deckers at this time.

Most of the front-engined AEC and Leyland double-deckers bought by BET firms were variants on the Regent and Titan, but AEC's lowheight Bridgemaster (City of Oxford, East Kent, East Yorkshire, South Wales and Western Welsh) and Renown (City of Oxford, East Yorkshire, North Western, South Wales and Western Welsh), and the Leyland-Albion Lowlander (East Midland, Ribble, Yorkshire Woollen) found favour with some companies.

The only other 'odd' front-engined double-deckers bought were the 50 AEC Routemasters with forward-entrance Park Royal bodies that were bought by Northern General in 1964-5.

The bodywork on front-engined double-deckers appears to have been a local company decision. Although BET had favoured builders, individual companies went to their favourite builders, or the local firm, or where they got the best price. So shorter-length double-deckers for BET fleets carried bodies by Beadle, Brush, Burlingham, East Lancs, Leyland, Metro-Cammell, Northern Coachbuilders, Northern Counties, Park Royal, Roe, Weymann and Willowbrook.

When 30ft double-deckers came along, the choice was more restricted, and while MCW (on AEC and Leyland) and Park Royal (on AEC) were the biggest builders and had the capacity to cope with BET orders among their commitments for London Transport and municipal fleets, and export business, some companies developed individual body styles that were built over a number of years. Most fondly-remembered are the Southdown 'Queen Marys', Leyland Titan PD3s with fully-fronted Northern Counties forward-entrance bodies, but Ribble also developed a full-fronted style, which was built initially by Burlingham and later by Metro-Cammell (and, less happily, by Alexander on Lowlander chassis). While Ribble also bought Atlanteans, Southdown resisted the lure of rear-engined double-deckers throughout BET days.

BET's desire for maximum-capacity buses to deal with the peaks that were now becoming even more pronounced encouraged Leyland to develop the rear-engined Atlantean, which allowed up to 78 seats and an entrance ahead of the front axle. The group fleets were keen customers for the Atlantean, and many went into BET companies right from the start of production in 1958-9. Two of the prototypes went to BET fleets, to James, Ammanford and Maidstone & District, and many of the early deliveries went to group companies. Atlantean customers were Devon General, East Midland, Gateshead, Maidstone & District, Mexborough & Swinton, Northern General, Potteries, Rhondda, Ribble, Sunderland District, Trent, Tynemouth, Tyneside, Wakefields, Western Welsh, Yorkshire Traction and Yorkshire Woollen.

One of the problems with the Atlantean was the initial lack of a proper lowheight version. A semi-lowheight version was offered, with some four-across seating at the rear of the upper deck, but this was not a satisfactory arrangement for passengers, and even when Leyland developed a true lowheight Atlantean, using a drop-centre rear axle, it was not as highly regarded as the similar Daimler Fleetline. The Fleetline found favour with City of Oxford, Maidstone & District, Mexborough & Swinton, North Western, Potteries, Trent, Tynemouth, Yorkshire Traction and Yorkshire Woollen. Some of these fleets were already operating Atlanteans, but for others the Fleetlines were their first rear-engined double-deckers.

With fewer bodybuilders in the market, bodies for BET on rear-engined double-deck chassis were more restricted. Metro-Cammell and Weymann were active from the launch of the Atlantean, and Alexander got a foot in the BET door with its bodies. Roe built rather uninspiring bodies on earlier Atlanteans, and Northern Counties built on Atlantean and Fleetline.

Buses got even longer in 1961 when 36ft by 8ft 2½in dimensions were legalised. Now single-deck buses could seat up to 53 or 54 passengers, and BET companies enthusiastically bought the new models. The two main chassis

South Wales was the first customer for AEC's lowheight Renown. No 1241 (304 ECY), a 3B3RA model of 1963, with 71-seat Park Royal body, at Port Talbot in October 1966. *R. L. Wilson*

Some BET Group companies were keen to buy Bristol and ECW products when they returned to the open market in the mid-1960s. East Midland No D512 (LAL 512E), a 1967 Bristol RELL6G with ECW 49-seat bus body, draws out of Mansfield garage in 1967. *Policy Transport Photographs*

Midland Red, which had done so much pioneering work with underfloor-engined single-deckers, tried the same principle with two experimental D10 double-deckers in the early 1960s. No 4944 (1944 HA), the 1961 version with 77-seat BMMO body, is seen at Stafford in 1971. The D10 anticipated models like the Volvo Citybus and Leyland Lion by 20 years. *Policy Transport Photographs*

were lengthened versions of the AEC Reliance and Leyland Leopard, which, in spite of their size and capacity, were still lighter than the early, shorter, underfloor-engined buses of a decade earlier. The Reliance was favoured by Aldershot & District, City of Oxford, Devon General, East Kent, East Midland, Hebble, Maidstone & District, Northern General, Potteries, South Wales, Sunderland District, Thomas and Yorkshire Woollen. The Leopard was bought by East Midland, East Yorkshire, Hebble, Maidstone & District, Northern General, Potteries, Ribble, South Wales, Southdown, Stratford Blue, Sunderland District, Trent, Western Welsh, Yorkshire Traction and Yorkshire Woollen. It will be seen that some fleets stuck to one or other model, while others bought both, often concentrating the different types at different garages.

The first bodies for 36ft-long single-deck buses were a rather clumsy-looking development of the BET style for shorter-length single-deckers, but soon a new classic was evolved to suit BET. It featured a new double-curvature windscreen that is still known as the BET screen on current deliveries, and distinctive front and back peaks which gave the body a crisp and modern look. The BET design was built by Marshall, Park Royal, Weymann and Willowbrook, and became a standard design that was bought by a wide range of operators. Alexander also built bodies for BET on 36ft Reliances and Leopards, but to its equally classic Y type design, most readily associated with the Scottish Bus Group.

In the mid-1960s the leading manufacturers introduced rear-engined single-deck chassis, but these seemed to be more suited to intense urban duties and the BET Group companies,

Dennis buses were rare in the BET Group, with Aldershot & District the largest customer. With Dennis chassis built within A&D's area, at Guildford, the choice was possibly less surprising. No 207 (LOU 35), seen at Reading in 1963, is a 1953 Dennis Lance K4 with East Lancs 56-seat lowbridge body. *A. J. Douglas/ Photobus*

Sheffield United Tours was the first customer for Plaxton's big-windowed Panorama body, and SUT continued to buy Panoramas for many years. Nos 331/3 (331/3 BWB) of 1962 have different chassis: No 331 is an AEC Reliance 2U3RA, and No 333 a Leyland Leopard PSU3/3RT. Both are 44-seaters, and are seen at Sheffield bus station in 1973. *R. L. Wilson*

wisely as it turned out, tended to stick to underfloor designs. Some did enter service — AEC Swifts with City of Oxford and East Midland; Daimler Roadliners with Black & White (coaches) and Potteries; Leyland Panthers with Maidstone & District, Northern General, Ribble and Thomas; Leyland Panther Cubs with Thomas. The best of the rear-engined single-deckers, the Bristol RE, only came on the open market in 1965, and in the later days of BET East Midland, North Western, Ribble, Southdown and Trent all bought examples.

Coaches figured largely in some BET fleets, and hardly at all in others. Some companies built up successful local private hire businesses, others offered day and afternoon tours and excursions, others operated extended tours in Britain and the Continent, and many had express services that required higher-specification vehicles.

As with the bus fleet, AEC and Leyland chassis were usually favoured for coaches, front-engined Regals and Tigers, then underfloor-engined Regal IVs and Reliances, and Tiger Cubs and Leopards. In the days when there were dozens of firms building coach bodies, BET fleets turned to the mainstream builders (Burlingham, Duple, Harrington, Leyland, Plaxton) as well as the more specialised firms (Bellhouse Hartwell, Windover). Then as the number of

A body manufacturer that barely got a glimpse of BET orders was Strachans, which built 30 of its Pacesaver bodies on Leyland Panther PSUR1/1R rear-engined chassis for Maidstone & District. No 3112 (LKT 112F) of 1968 is seen at Hastings shortly after entering service. *R. A. Jenkinson*

The first underfloor-engined chassis generally available from AEC and Leyland were heavyweights which offered poor fuel consumption. In the economy-conscious days of the 1950s these were quickly succeeded by lighter-weight models like the AEC Reliance and Leyland Tiger Cub. This early underfloor-engined single-decker is a Devon General Leyland Royal Tiger PSU1/9 with Willowbrook 43-seat body, No SL638 (MTT 638) seen in 1953 at the Strand, Torquay.
L. F. Folkard

Three of the more 'glamorous' BET companies went for full-fronted 30ft-long forward-entrance double-deckers in the late 1950s. Ribble and Southdown chose Leyland Titans, but East Kent went for the AEC Regent V LD3RA with stylish Park Royal bodywork. PFN 845, a 72-seater, was new in 1958.
Ian Allan Library

coachbuilders reduced, orders were concentrated on a much smaller number — usually Duple, Harrington and Plaxton, with some individuality expressed by specifying Alexander, Park Royal or Weymann bodies.

Lighter-weight coaches, popular with independent operators for hire and touring work, did not generally fit in with BET's type of operation, but Bedfords, Commers and Fords were bought by several firms, usually with bodies by the mainstream coachbuilders.

As a major potential customer, the BET Group had immense buying power, and used its strength to influence the chassis manufacturers, particularly AEC and Leyland, and the small group of bodybuilders who relied heavily on BET work. Unlike Tilling, which used its in-house builders, Bristol and ECW, to produce a highly-standardised range of types tailored to the group's needs — which on many occasions led to compromise purchases — BET used its position to influence the types that were on the market, and allowed its companies more freedom in specifying their buses. At the end of the day it was important that the bus company made money, and BET seemed happy to give its companies freedom to buy with the group or to negotiate their own deals. Many companies, as we have seen, toed the party line, and others confidently went their own way.

A later style of Plaxton Panorama body on Ribble No 792 (ARN 792C), a 1965 Leyland Leopard PSU3/3RT with 49-seat body, at Keswick in July 1967. *R. L. Wilson*

One consequence of the formation of NBC was the rationalising of company areas between former Tilling and BET companies. The transfer of United's Carlisle garage, and vehicles, to Ribble, led to the unusual sight of a Bristol LS in Ribble colours. No 262 (632 CHN) is a 1956 LS6G with ECW 45-seat bus body, seen at Carlisle bus station in August 1969 alongside a Ribble two-door Bristol RELL. *R. L. Wilson*

Ribble No 228 (FRN 228F), a 1968 Bristol RELL6L with two-door ECW 41-seat body, at Fleetwood in 1971. Ribble was one of the BET fleets that recognised the value of the RELL bus, though the all-conquering Leyland National would shortly become the standard single-deck model. *P. Eckersley/Photobus*

Midland Red was able to
continue producing its own
single-deck models right to
1970. The final BMMO-built
models were 36ft-long single-
deckers. No 5898
(MHA 898F) is an example of
the penultimate type, the
45-seat S22 (built in 1968)
with BMMO bodywork.
Ian Allan Library

▲ 5. The Later Years

The passenger decline after the heights of the early 1950s hit the
bus industry badly. Tilling, London Transport and the Scottish
Group, all state-owned, were resigned to the idea that such
decline was unfortunate, and economies would be made to try to
deal with the situation and efforts made to generate new
business, but what was being provided was a public service.

BET was a rather different organisation. As we have seen, it
was moving away from its roots in public transport and was
fast becoming a successful worldwide business with a
responsibility to its shareholders. It could see the trends and
these were a cause of great concern. Between 1956 and 1966
the number of bus passengers fell by 30% at the same time as
costs were constantly increasing. Fuel duty represented an
immense burden for bus operators, and these extra costs were
reflected in higher bus fares. BET reckoned that, in 10 of its

companies selected at random, an average of 50% of the
routes and 30% of the mileage were run at a loss. The total
number of unremunerative miles run in a year by these 10
companies alone came to 78 million.

Rural routes were the first to feel the pinch, and in the later
part of the 1950s many were cut back or withdrawn altogether.
This caused an increase in rural car ownership, and so the
vicious circle continued. Driver-only services coupled with
lighter and more economical buses helped the situation in
many marginal areas. In the urban areas, use of high-capacity
buses helped spread the costs.

Labour costs were rising disproportionately, and in an
industry where labour represented 70% of total costs, this was
a serious problem. Driver-only buses were one solution, but
the unions insisted that these should be restricted to buses on
unremunerative routes and limited the seating capacity.

As a whole, BET saw its passenger numbers drop by 31%
between 1956 and 1967, while the average number of buses
fell by only 7.7%, from 12,161 to 11,221. The problem was
that capacity was needed for the peaks, and many buses were
unused between peaks.

Then there were the first rumblings of significant changes in
the bus industry — the creation of the first Passenger
Transport Executives (PTEs) being the move that would most
affect BET, with profitable operations in the northeast, the
Manchester/Cheshire area and the West Midlands potentially
at risk. It seemed likely that the hearts would be ripped out of
profitable BET companies, leaving the local authorities to pick
up the cost of the rest. 'Surely', BET Chairman John Spencer
Wills wrote in an annual report, 'after decades of service to
public road passenger transport, starting in the earliest days of
the electric tramcar, your company deserves better than that.'

In a way this was the area boards of the postwar years all
over again, but this time BET was not prepared to fight, and in
November 1967, following an approach by the state-owned
Transport Holding Company, it decided to sell its
shareholdings in its bus companies for £35 million. The
purchase was completed early in 1968, and allowed the new
National Bus Company to be created, bringing together the
BET and Tilling fleets in England and Wales to form a
massive new grouping.

It is tempting to speculate that BET was glad to have the
opportunity to sell its UK bus interests for such a good price.
For years the bus companies in England and Wales had

produced useful profits (as of course many of them did for the state, where there had been a railway shareholding), but in 1967 BET's bus income showed a net return of only 5.4%, while it was earning considerably healthier returns from what were fast becoming its main interests — TV rental, relay and broadcasting, freight transport and construction. BET reckoned that the £35 million offered by THC would not be matched in compensation following compulsory acquisition, and that — as indeed happened — there would be more PTEs in its profitable areas. For BET, enough was enough.

North Western, with a strong Bristol bias in the days before Bristol passed into state control, was another enthusiastic customer for the RELL, and continued to buy the model into NBC days. Among its last, before the North Western company was split up, was No 382 (SJA 382K), a 1972 RELL6L with 49-seat ECW body, at Northwich bus station in 1972. *Policy Transport Photographs*

For the first years under NBC control vehicle orders continued along existing lines, and company liveries and fleetnames remained unchanged. This is Yorkshire Woollen No 136 (3157 WE), a Leyland Titan PD2/30 with 59-seat Roe bodywork, new to the railway-owned Sheffield C fleet in 1958, and acquired by Yorkshire Woollen following the break-up of the Sheffield Joint Omnibus Committee in 1970. *H. J. Black*

One of the more bizarre consequences of the formation of the National Bus Company and the consequent rationalisations, was the sight of Bristol Lodekkas in Southdown colours. Former Brighton, Hove & District Bristol FS6B ENJ 68C, new in 1965 with ECW 60-seat body, at Old Steine, Brighton, in 1973 wearing Southdown-BH&D livery as No 2068. *Policy Transport Photographs*

North Western did not survive for long under NBC ownership. It was broken up and split between Selnec PTE, Crosville, Trent and National Travel (North West). Symbolic of the changes are these two ex-North Western AEC Renown 3B3RAs with Park Royal 74-seat bodies, both by then in the Crosville fleet, though still carrying 'On Hire to North Western' stickers. No DAA515 (VDB 980) in full Crosville green stands alongside No DAA504 (VDB 967) still in North Western red/cream. *J. G. Carroll*

▲ 6. The Legacy of BET

BET was very different to Tilling, and each organisation brought its strengths to the new National Bus Company after it started to trade in 1969. BET's more aggressive and commercial approach matched Tilling's views on standardisation, central control and public service. Although the first years were uneasy as staff from different backgrounds were mixed through the new organisation, and there may have been some reservations about the wisdom of a 20,000-plus-vehicle bus company, there is no doubt that BET held its own in the new set-up.

There were significant changes to the structure of the industry under the new NBC. Companies that had survived as rather unnatural neighbours now found themselves merged, and some even disappeared altogether.

Aldershot & District was merged with its Tilling neighbour, Thames Valley, to create the Thames Valley & Aldershot Omnibus Co Ltd, whose buses wore the unusual Alder Valley fleetname.

Black & White was renamed National Travel (South West) in 1973 at which point the Greenslades business was also absorbed. Samuelson and Timpson were absorbed into National Travel (South East) in 1973. Sheffield United was taken over by National Travel (North East) in 1973.

City of Oxford took control of Tilling's South Midland company in a logical move.

Devon General was taken over by Western National in 1970, the same year it absorbed the Exeter Corporation bus fleet.

East Midland assumed responsibility for the management of Mansfield District in 1972.

North Western, with more than half of its mileage in the Selnec PTE area, was disbanded in 1972, and was split between the PTE, Crosville and Trent, while its coaches went to National Travel (North West).

The Northern General group of companies managed to co-exist with Tyneside (later Tyne & Wear) PTE, and painted its buses operating in the PTE area in yellow.

Ribble took over United Auto's Carlisle area in 1969.

South Wales absorbed Neath & Cardiff, Thomas Bros and United Welsh in 1971, and the Western Welsh garages at Neath and Haverfordwest in 1972.

Southdown assumed control for Tilling's Brighton, Hove & District company in 1969, but this was wound up in 1974.

Trent took control of Tilling's Notts & Derby company in 1969, and the Buxton and Matlock garages of North Western in 1972.

Western Welsh took over Rhondda in 1971.

Yorkshire Woollen became part of the West Riding group of companies (the independent West Riding company had been bought by THC in 1967). Hebble became Yorkshire Woollen's coaching unit, later becoming part of National Travel (North East); Hebble's bus services passed to the Halifax JOC.

East Kent, East Yorkshire, Maidstone & District, Midland Red, Potteries and Yorkshire Traction were left largely untouched — for the time being anyway. Later changes would rip the commercial heart out of Midland Red (as anticipated by BET), and all the remaining companies faced the trauma of privatisation and deregulation in the 1980s.

As the following table shows, BET Group companies ranged from just 15 buses to over 1,800, with huge increases in the 15 years after 1938, when fleets had often reached their optimum size.

It is tempting to wonder why BET maintained so many fleets, when in areas like Yorkshire, South Wales, and even southeast England, economies could have been made by merging companies, or at least rationalising operations. That BET chose not to do this is partly explained by its training structure, which gave managers the opportunity to prove themselves in smaller companies before moving through the ranks to the biggest companies.

The BET Fleet

Company	1938	1952-3	1965
Aldershot & District	242	347	285
Midland Red	1,228	1,803	1,780
Black & White	70	81	
Caledonian	108		
Chatham & District	44	53	
Devon General	226	310	278
East Kent	546	611	610
East Midland	150	203	224
East Yorkshire	192	282	246
Gateshead	67*	72	68
Hastings Tramways	58+	49+	
Hebble	70	84	73
James, Ammanford		38	
Maidstone & District	552	816	772
Mexborough & Swinton	39**	45**	50
Neath & Cardiff		32	31
North Western	521	562	553
Northern General	385	653	624
City of Oxford	171	247	223
Potteries	252	500	506
Rhondda	123	211	164
Ribble	1,045	1,155	1,093
Sheffield United Tours		95	103
South Wales	285	312	333
Southdown	676	919	897
Stratford Blue	20	30	44
Sunderland District	81	111	95
Trent	363	431	380
Tynemouth	50	67	73
Tyneside	17	21	17
Wakefields	15	19	15
Western Welsh	431	610	570
Yorkshire Traction	303	375	339
Yorkshire Woollen	259	308	268

*   Tramcars
+   Trolleybuses
** In 1938 M&S owned 36 trolleybuses and 3 motorbuses; in 1952-3 M&S owned 39 trolleybuses and 6 motorbuses

Source: The Little Red Book *for the years indicated*

Further Reading

The many books covering aspects of the operations of the BET Group reflect its importance in the history of the British bus industry. The books I found particularly valuable in researching this title were: *A National Bus Company Album* by Ray Stenning (Viewfinder, 1979); *British Buses Before 1945* by John Aldridge (Ian Allan, 1995); *British Buses Since 1945* by Stephen Morris (Ian Allan, 1995); *Bus Operators: 2 — NBC, Antecedents & Formation* by Stewart J. Brown (Ian Allan, 1983); *Fifteen Years On* by G. E. Mingay (BET, 1973), *Golden Age of Buses* by Charles F. Klapper (Routledge & Kegan Paul, 1978); *The Bristol Story, Part One — 1908-1951* by Alan Townsin (Venture Publications, 1996); *The History of British Bus Services* by John Hibbs (David & Charles, 1968); *The Official ABC Coach Guide for Great Britain*, *The Sixth Decade* by Roger Fulford (BET, 1956) and *The Years before National* by Ray Stenning (Fleetline Books, 1982). There are also a number of histories of individual BET Group companies, mostly published by Venture and its predecessor, Transport Publishing Co. Although a number of these books are out of print, they may be found at rallies and other enthusiast events, or obtained from specialist dealers.